après the mango season
Zoe Rosenthal

I0418261

for all you lovers, and for the ones who taught me
sweetness

contents

chapter 1: the mango blooms

chapter 2: the mango falls

chapter 3: the bruised mango

chapter 4: the mango softens

the mango blooms

india after rain

he walks in
and the air smells of wet earth
the sky still holding
its last drops of monsoon
i watch him, smile like a secret
that the clouds whispered only to me
his hands speak
in the language of mango trees
and jasmine blooms
i never knew i wanted to learn
every laugh he gives
rains warmth into my chest
i bloom where i thought i had only dust
i fall, like rain falling on hot rooftops
soft
unafraid
completely undone
and i am india after rain
alive + swept into his sweetness

mango season

he hands me a mango
ripe and heavy
juice dripping
and i taste summer
in the curve of his smile
we sit under the tree
sunlight tangled in his hair
the air sweet with fruit
and the promise of something
soft and slow
between us
every bite
is a little surrender
every glance
is a little falling
and i am full
of mangoes
and him

chai & old treasures

he lifts a delicate cup
and i watch
steam curl
like his smile
chai warms our hands
and something quieter
spreads between us
we wander through shops
that smell of antique wood and dust
time stacked on shelves—
brass lamps, carved boxes,
clocks holding their breath
he lifts an old lamp
smiles like it was made for me
and i believe him
i touch a wooden box
its lid smooth from other hands
his fingers brush mine
and the world tilts
just enough
jasmine and sandalwood
cling to the air, to us
every doorway we pass
every object we return
feels like a small rehearsal
for choosing

by the time the tea cools
i am already falling
not fast, not loud—
but certain
like something meant
to be kept

chicago rain

he talks
and the streets of chicago
fold into my chest
his laugh carries
reminds me of spices i have only smelled
in dreams of india
i watch him sip coffee
winter wind tangling his hair
and i fall
soft as snow
soft as monsoon
his hand brushes mine
and suddenly
i am everywhere
and nowhere
but here with him
he smiles
in case you didn't know
chicago rains taste like india

softcore

california sun
spills across the room
like it has nowhere else to be
he laughs—
the sound loose, unguarded
salt still on his skin
the ocean keeps folding itself
into the afternoon
as if repetition could make it last
light catches in his hair
rests there
longer than it should
i give in
the way water does—
not breaking, not asking
just staying
where it's warm
every word he says
moves slowly through me
unhurried, sure
this is how it happens:
slowly—
the body
loosening
its grip
i count the spaces between our fingers
like prayers

each touch a promise
of falling again
and again

saltwater honey

the tide hums low against the shore
and you stand there
like the ocean
just agreed
to worship you
salt clings to the curve of your wrist
i wonder
what it would taste like
if i were brave enough
to find out
you look at me
with that quiet curiosity
that feels like
an invitation
or a warning
i can't tell which
warm, unsteady
like honey melting
in summer heat

midnight train

the train hums beneath our feet
i watch your shadow
curl against the window
and wonder
if it knows my heart
is already half in your lap
the lights blur past
your hand
brushes against mine
for a heartbeat
the train keeps going
as if it knows
how easily
i could stay

perfume of rain

the scent of wet earth
clings to your collar
i breathe it in
as if it might teach me
what comes next
the rain has stopped
but the air holds on—
cool, waiting
i think of summers
we never learned how to enter
days that stayed just out of reach
you stand close
not touching
between us
the space smells like rain
and almost

fingers intertwined

no one else sees it—
the quiet claim
of skin on skin
i think about
how much can be promised
with so little
how letting go
will someday
hurt more
than holding on does now

monsoon pulse

your voice
moves through me
like the first rumble
of monsoon thunder—
quiet,
impossible to ignore
you say my name
and something in me
opens
like wet earth
after the first rain
drinking in
every syllable
you give
your laugh
brushes my skin
soft as humidity before the storm
i am waiting, heart trembling
for the downpour of you

lebanon

he smiles
and the sun lingers
in his eyes
but never stays
i reach
and he drifts
like jasmine on the wind
sweet
but just out of reach
every word he doesn't say
every touch he withholds
is a little ache
that tastes like honey
and hesitation

the mango falls

the unsaid

your silence
arrived
before your leaving
days before
you said the words
i already felt
the door
in your chest
closing
i held my breath
waiting
for something soft
to return
but you only offered
shadows
and half-smiles
the last thing
you ever gave me
was nothing said out loud

alternate lifetimes

i see us elsewhere—
waking into the same light
learning each other slowly
there are mornings
that belong to us
in another life
where love is not careful
but here
you do not reach
you do not fight for me
or bend for us
you let the distance
do its work
i am left holding
what we almost were
wondering how many lives
it takes
for someone
to choose

departures

they embrace as if the world will end
i sit, heart tugging, luggage at my feet
imagining someone waiting for me too

bruised fruit

i hold the mango
you left
on my counter
days ago
its skin
is softening
collapsing inward
like something
forgotten
i touch it
and feel
the bruise
beneath the surface—
tender,
dark,
spreading
i did not realize
you were teaching me
how love wastes away
when left unheld

aftertaste

you linger
in the quiet
like fruit left
too long
on the counter
sweet at first—
then something
turns
the room holds it
that soft, wrong note
i keep tasting
grief settles
on the tongue
slow, unmistakable
and does not leave

empty walls

i come home
and the apartment is silent
the hum of life
that should feel like freedom
feels like weight
solitude was supposed to be air
a place to breathe
but these walls
only echo the absence of you
i pour myself tea
i light candles
i try to fill the quiet
but it stays
a hollow reminder
that freedom
is heavy
when it is lonely

reincarnation

i close my eyes
and imagine you
tiny again
soft as sunlight
in my arms
this time
i carry you longer
i believe love like this
cannot be ended,
only transformed
so i wait
i hope
one day
your spirit will return to me
in a body
i can love
and hold
again

his sweater

i find your sweater
in the back
of my closet
the fabric still holding
the faintest trace
of you
i pull it
over my head
and the memory
wraps itself
around my ribs
tight, familiar, unwanted
i stand in the mirror
wearing a ghost
and wonder
how something
that once warmed me
could now feel
cold

the sink

your toothbrush
still sits
in the cup
beside mine
i tell myself
i will throw it away
tomorrow
but tomorrow
keeps slipping
out of reach
grief
is a slow undoing
it starts
with small things—
your favorite coffee cup
a song you hummed
a brush stroke
and ends
with me
standing at the sink
staring at pieces
you left behind

messages you will never read

words i will never send
pile like snow
on the edges of my phone
each letter
a small confession
a tiny surrender
apologies
i did not earn
questions
that learned better
and i let them sit
unsaid
unsent
as if silence
is something
i am practicing

gate 32

i watch people run
toward those
who waited for them
arms thrown
around shoulders
laughter sharp
with relief
i sit alone
my boarding pass
a flimsy reminder
that moving forward
is not the same
as healing
the speaker calls
i rise
carrying
nothing
but what i could not
leave behind

fading photographs

i keep your photographs
in drawers that smell of cedar
i touch them
softly
as if my hands
could pull you back
from the past
but you
are already gone
and i am still decimated

citrus

the sheets are cold
and the air
smells like citrus
and someone else's life
i sit at the edge
of a bed
meant for two
but holding only me
and your absence
i try to sleep
but the room
keeps shifting
like it knows
i am trying
to forget
night after night
i leave the bedside lamp on
hoping the light will soften the ache

the bruised mango

the anatomy of depression

sometimes i feel
like a photograph
left in a drawer
the edges fading
beside unworn pearls
objects meant
for another life
or like mango trees
in india
no one waters
their roots
remember rain
their branches
still reach
but the fruit
drops early
soft
before it's ready

heavy water

some mornings
even the shower
hurts
the water
falls against my skin
like it is trying
to wash me
back into someone
i no longer remember
i stand there, counting droplets
as if they might
give me back
my own name
but depression
turns everything to heavy water
and i cannot float
no matter
how long
i stay beneath the heat

static

there is a buzzing
behind my ribs
a low static
i cannot turn off
it crackles
through conversations
through sunlight
through the softest moments
until everything
sounds distorted
sometimes
i wonder
what silence
used to feel like
before the noise
moved in
and made a home
in my chest

unfinished

depression
takes my legs
before i can stand
and my words
before i can speak
the bed becomes
a gravity i cannot fight
a blank page
a mirror that refuses
to open
i want to rise
i want to write
but wanting
feels miles away
lifetimes away
my mind is asking for mercy
today
breathing is the only poem i can finish

grocery aisle

i stand frozen
between the fruit
and the canned goods
a simple list
in my hand
that feels
like a foreign language
someone laughs
near the bakery
the sound
cracks something
inside my chest
even in a room
full of people
i hear the hum
of my own fear
every sound
too close
every pause
too loud
i stare at the oranges
trying to remember
what hunger
is supposed
to feel like

the world moves
around me
bright and effortless
while i stay
caught
like a forgotten item
on a shelf

the lost day

today slipped
through my fingers
before i even
opened my eyes
i blinked
and the sun
was already
taking its exit bow
across my window
hours went missing
without sound
i cannot name
what filled them
only the weight
of staying
maybe tomorrow
will return
what i misplaced

conversations between me and me

me:
do you remember
waking without dragging yourself
through every hour?

you:
i do
but you feel like a stranger
a body you once knew

me:
why are you so quiet?
i am heavy
my bones forget how to move

you:
i see you
and i miss you
how easily you breathed
how the world fit inside your hands

me:
will you come back?

you:
one day
we will walk together

and you will remember
how to be yourself again

me:
for now?

you:
listen
to the echo of me
inside you

a room in my chest

my heart is full
of vintage, sad furniture
worn velvet chairs
that sag under the weight
of years i cannot name
dust gathers in corners
where sunlight used to live
and every step
echoes hollow
across floors
that remember better days
i try to sweep it clean
but the pieces stay
and i sit among them
learning to breathe
in a room
that is mine
even when it aches

blue hour

the sky bruises
into evening
soft purple, soft blue
soft ache
i sit by the window
watching the light leave
as if i might disappear
with it
there is a moment
just before night
when the world holds
its breath
i pretend
the stillness
is meant for me
a quiet space
to rest
my tired mind

the mango softens

safety

safety feels like
stepping into a warm bath
the water holds me
without asking
for anything
my skin remembers
it is allowed to relax
my heart remembers
it is allowed to rest
i sink
and the world softens
around me
for the first time
i am just me
and it is enough

first light

sun breaks
across the windowsill
not all at once—
just enough
to be noticed
i sit up
slowly
the room
still holding
its breath
coffee warms my hands
the sheets remember me
i don't call it hope
but something in me
stays

warm bread

he hands me a slice
still steaming
from the oven
and for a moment
the world feels small
and kind
we eat in silence
but the silence
is not sharp
like it used to be
it is soft
like dough rising
like something
becoming whole
in its own sweet time

new roots

i water my plants
and watch them reach
for light
they do not question
whether they deserve it
i sit beside them
and try to learn
how to grow
without apology
how to soften
without fear
i tell myself
i am allowed
to root again
even after storms
have snapped me
in half

the shape of joy

i am learning
that joy is a slow, quiet unfold
a breath
i didn't know
i was holding
released
it lives
in the small things—
clean sheets
a friend's laugh
the gentle way
sunlight rests
on my arm
tiny reminders
that life
is still offering
its hand

becoming

there is softness
in my face
i thought i had lost
grief carved me
into someone new
but this version
is learning
how to breathe
without breaking
how to build
without burning
i touch my cheek
and whisper—
you made it

to my future love

i dreamt of you
all my life
soft love
that folds around me
like sunlight through curtains
our children will be
full of light
running through rooms
laughing and spilling dreams
and i will make scones
with them on slow sunday mornings
they will roll their eyes
at how often you kiss me
but i will only kiss you
more
in each lifetime

interracial love

our love is quiet rebellion
it blooms between us
bright and tender
and yet
i feel the weight of eyes
that do not understand
their whispers
cut deeper than absence
their stares
try to shrink what is vast
and beautiful
and still
i hold your hand proudly
because the world
cannot
will not
touch this

mango softens

the bruises
have not left me
they sit
like small moons
under my skin
but even fruits
ripen
after falling
i am learning
to trust
the slow sweetness
returning
to my own hands
i am not
what hurt me
i am what survived
and softened
and sweetened anyway

morning call

she calls
just to ask
if i've eaten
and somehow
i begin to cry
her voice
wraps around me
like a blanket
old and warm
reminding me
that love
does not always
take
it often
returns
sometimes
healing begins
with someone asking
have you had breakfast

balconies

i step onto the balcony
and the air
is cool
against my skin
cars hum below
birds argue
in the trees
life
moves on
without waiting
for me
and yet
tonight
i feel caught
in its rhythm
a quiet reminder
that even after long winters
the world still opens
and so do i

moonlight sonata

the piano begins
softly
as if afraid
to wake something
keys catching light
from the window
your hands
used to rest here—
not playing
just listening
the melody moves
in small circles
returning
without insisting
outside
the night holds still
inside
something loosens
its grip
i don't reach for the past
but it leans toward me
anyway
for a moment
the dark
feels arranged
into meaning

quiet anniversary

today marks a year
since the world
dropped me
to my knees
i do not celebrate
but i do sit
with myself
i make tea
and sip it slowly
letting the steam
touch my face
like a small blessing
here i am
hands warm
breathing gently
in a room
that did not exist back then
and that is enough to call a victory

the softest part

i have spent years
armored
against loss
and longing
the quiet ache
of being human
but healing
is not becoming harder
it is learning
where to soften
the day ends
and the sky
bruises into evening—
pink, then fading
i breathe
and let the light
leave without chasing it
to stay open
not clenched
to keep my hands
open
to let love
touch the softest part of me
without flinching
even as the dark
settles in

remember—
that even endings
can be beautiful
i always declare
i have had the best mango of my life
until
i taste
the next one

About the Author

Zoe Rosenthal is a poet whose work explores love, loss, and recovery through sensory, intimate lyricism. She holds a master's degree in criminal justice and crime analysis from Boston University, where she developed a deep interest in patterns, perception, and the unseen architecture of human behavior. *après the mango season* is her debut poetry collection, tracing desire, grief, and healing through the lifecycle of sweetness. She believes poetry offers a way of knowing that exists beyond measurement—where feeling becomes its own form of truth.